AF263698

DEDICATED TO MY CHILDREN. MAY YOU
ALWAYS REACH FOR THE STARS!
- DADDY

Space Skunks
Copyright © 2020 by Josh Potler
Art Direction by Garon Levine

All rights reserved. This book or any portion thereof
may not be reproduced or used in any manner whatsoever
without the express written permission of the publisher.
To request permissions, please contact joshpotler@gmail.com.

Printed in the United States of America
Florida Lis Inc.

ISBN: 978-1-953399-84-7

Space
Skunks
BY JOSH
POTLER

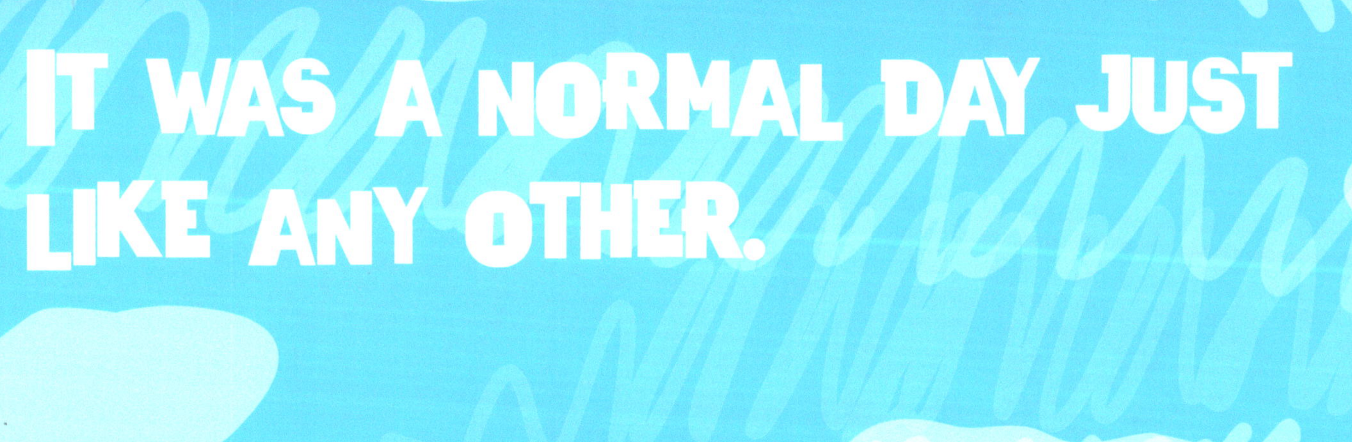

IT WAS A NORMAL DAY JUST LIKE ANY OTHER.

After training for many hours at space school...
Preparing their flight suits...
Practicing how to fly...
And learning to work as a team...

SPACE SCHOOL

STINKERS, SMELLY, AND STENCH ATE THEIR DINNER AND GOT READY FOR BED.

THE THREE SKUNKS BRUSHED THEIR TEETH, COMBED THEIR SHINY HAIR, AND LAID DOWN TO SLEEP.

WHEN IT CAME TIME TO REST, THE GREAT BALL OF BRIGHTNESS DID NOT GO DOWN!

SQUAWK! SQUAWK!
SCREECHED THE PHEASANT
PHONE! "SKUNK SQUAD,
REPORT FOR DUTY!"

MOMENTS LATER, STINKERS, SMELLY, AND STENCH STOOD AT ATTENTION, READY FOR THEIR ORDERS FROM SERGEANT SKUNK!

"Skunk Squad! The Earth is caught on a star and has stopped spinning!" Sergeant Skunk announced.

"IT IS YOUR DUTY TO FLY TO SPACE AND START THE EARTH SPINNING ONCE AGAIN. YOU MUST BRING BACK NIGHTTIME, SO THAT WE CAN ALL GO TO SLEEP," HE CONTINUED.

CONFIDENTIAL
SKUNK SQUAD
Your Duty
CONFIDENTIAL

EXIT

THE SKUNKS AGREED THAT NOW WAS THE TIME FOR THE THREE TO BECOME REAL SPACE SKUNKS!

Start the countdown Sergeant Skunk began,
"10, 9, 8, 7, 6, 5, 4, 3, 2, 1 . . .
Blast Off!"

Blast Off!
1
2
3
4
5
6
7
8
9
10

LAUNCH

MOMENTS LATER THE SPACE SKUNKS ENTERED ZERO GRAVITY IN OUTER SPACE. THEY ADMIRED THE MOON, THE STARS, AND THE PLANETS THAT SURROUNDED THEM.

WITH ALL THEIR MIGHT AND THEIR LOOPING LASSOS, THE SKUNKS WERE ABLE TO PLUCK THE STAR FROM ITS PLACE.

USING THEIR SPECIAL SKUNK SPRAY, THE SQUAD ZIPPED AROUND THE EARTH TUGGING POWERFULLY UNTIL IT STARTED SPINNING ONCE AGAIN!

A SUCCESSFUL SPIN BROUGHT NIGHTTIME BACK TO EARTH AND STINKERS, SMELLY, AND STENCH FLEW BACK DOWN TO RECEIVE THEIR HERO'S WELCOME.

THE SPACE SKUNKS SAFELY LANDED TO A VERY EXHAUSTED AND SLEEPY CELEBRATION...

WITH NIGHTTIME BACK ONCE AGAIN, THE THREE WERE OFF TO BED, TO SNUGGLE IN THEIR WARM TREE DEN WITH DREAMS OF SPACE AND THEIR NEXT ADVENTURE, WHEN THE SUN WOULD RISE AGAIN!